**Genre:** fiction

**Setting:** Sylvan and Tiburon, South Carolina, 1964

**Point of View:** first person

**Themes:** coming-of-age, self-discovery, resilience, family issues (abandonment, mental and physical abuse, rejection), persisting in love, coping with loss, racism, guilt, redemption

**Conflict:** person vs. person, person vs. self, person vs. society

**Style:** narrative

**Tone:** reflective, yearning

**Date of First Publication:** 2002

## Summary

Lily Owens, the narrator and protagonist, lives with her harsh, inattentive father, T. Ray, on a peach farm near Sylvan, South Carolina. Her mother, Deborah, died under mysterious circumstances when Lily was four years old, and T. Ray has told Lily she is responsible for her mother's accidental death. Lily's black nanny, Rosaleen, is the primary maternal figure in Lily's life for the ten years following Deborah's death. Rosaleen is jailed and severely beaten when she attempts to register to vote, and Lily rescues her. The two decide to seek refuge in Tiburon, the town whose name is written on the back of Deborah's black Virgin Mary picture. There they find refuge and healing in the home of a black beekeeper, August Boatwright, and her two sisters. Lily discovers the secrets of her mother's past, finds security with her new "mothers," and attains redemption from the guilt of her mother's death.

## About the Author

Sue Monk Kidd was born and raised in Sylvester, Georgia. Demonstrating an early desire to write, Kidd began writing stories and keeping a prolific journal as an adolescent. Two books she read as a teenager, Thoreau's spiritual memoir *Walden* and Kate Chopin's novel *The Awakening*, influenced her greatly. Upon graduating from Texas Christian University in 1970 with a B.S. degree in nursing, Kidd worked as a registered nurse and instructor in college nursing classes.

Shortly before her thirtieth birthday, she enrolled in writing classes. Her career as a freelance writer began when an article of hers was accepted for publication by *Guideposts* magazine. She concentrated primarily on inspirational personal experience articles and eventually became a Contributing Editor at *Guideposts*. Her first book was a spiritual memoir, *God's Joyful Surprise* (1987). Other nonfiction works include *All Things Are Possible* (1988), *When the Heart Waits* (1990), *The Dance of the Dissident Daughter* (1996), *A Luminous Presence* (2005), and *Firstlight* (2006), a collection of her early writings on spirituality.

Following her enrollment in a graduate writing course at Emory University, Kidd began to write and publish short stories in small literary journals. She expanded her short story "The Secret Life of Bees" into a full-length novel, and it was published in 2002.

*The Secret Life of Bees* went on to sell more than 5.5 million copies, has been published in more than 20 languages, and was listed on the *New York Times* bestseller list for approximately 80 weeks. The novel was named the 2004 Book Sense paperback of the year, and "Good Morning America" chose it for the "Read This!" Book Club. The book is widely taught in high school and college classes, has been produced on stage by The American Place Theatre, and is being adapted into a movie by Focus Features. Her second novel, *The Mermaid Chair*, was published in 2005.

Kidd serves on the Poets and Writers, Inc. advisory board, has received several awards for her short stories and nonfiction articles, and is the recipient of the 2004 inaugural Literature to Life award from the American Place Theatre. In addition, she is Writer in Residence at Phoebe Pember House in Charleston, South Carolina. She resides in Charleston with her husband Sanford (Sandy), with whom she has two adult children, Bob and Ann.

# Characters

**Lily Owens:** 14-year-old girl who struggles with guilt over her mother's death; lives with her cruel, negligent father; strives to understand issues such as racism, religion, and maturation; finds refuge for herself and Rosaleen in the home of the eccentric Boatwright sisters

**T. Ray Owens:** Lily's mean-spirited father, whose insensitivity and punishment make Lily's life miserable; runs a peach farm

**Deborah Fontanel Owens:** Lily's mother, whose mysterious death haunts Lily and is the reason she chooses to go to Tiburon

**Rosaleen Daise:** black nanny who has been the primary maternal figure in Lily's life since her mother's death; victim of vicious racist attack; journeys to Tiburon with Lily

**August Boatwright:** beekeeper; strong, religious, compassionate; gives Lily information about her mother and helps her find redemption from the past and hope for the future; organized the Daughters of Mary

**June Boatwright:** teacher; plays mournful music on her cello; initially rejects Lily but comes to love her

**May Boatwright:** consumed with empathy for anyone who suffers; retreats to her "wailing wall" when life becomes too intense; becomes Rosaleen's best friend; commits suicide

**Zachary Lincoln Taylor (Zach):** black teenager who works for August; hardworking, ambitious; forms close relationship with Lily; unfairly jailed because of a racist incident

**Neil:** black principal; in love with and wants to marry June

**Brother Gerald:** white racist minister at Lily's church in Sylvan

**Avery "Shoe" Gaston:** white racist police officer who takes Rosaleen to jail

**Franklin Posey:** white racist; most vicious of the three men who attack Rosaleen

**The Daughters of Mary (and one son):** Queenie, Violet, Lunelle, Mabelee, Cressie, Sugar-Girl, and Otis Hill, with the Boatwrights, celebrate the Black Madonna

**Clayton Forrest:** lawyer in Tiburon; friend to Zach and the Boatwrights

**Becca Forrest:** Clayton's daughter; becomes Lily's friend

# Background Information

The following information will enhance students' understanding of the novel.

1. The practice of beekeeping and the roles of bees in a colony correlate with events and people in the novel. Each colony consists of one queen bee, a few thousand drones (males), and a large population of worker bees (sterile females). The queen's primary function is reproduction, and her average productive life is 2–3 years. She mates with several drones outside of the hive and may produce up to 250,000 eggs per year, both fertilized and unfertilized. When an older queen's production begins to decrease, queen cells are fed royal jelly. If a queen dies suddenly, a new queen is produced from existing worker bee larvae. The main function of the drones is to fertilize the queen's eggs, but only a small percentage actually do this. A drone dies instantly after mating. Because they perform no useful work, the worker bees drive the drones out of the hive when cold weather begins, and they are left to die. The worker bees are the smallest, most numerous inhabitants of the colony. They clean the hive, feed the larvae, care for the Queen, produce honey, guard the entrance, and cool and ventilate the hive with their wings. (http://maarec.cas.psu.edu/bkCD/HBBiology/colony_org.html [Web site active at time of publication.])

2. The term "Black Madonna" or "Black Virgin" applies to any dark-skinned statue or painting of the Virgin Mary. Numerous such representations, e.g., Our Lady of Czestochowa, are found in Europe; a few are located in museums, but most are in churches or shrines. One shrine to the Black Madonna is located in Doylestown, Pennsylvania. The Black Madonna of Breznichar portrayed in *The Secret Life of Bees* is fictional. The Web site http://www.google.com/answers/threadview?id=480148 (active at time of publication) gives several links referring to Black Madonnas.

3. The Civil Rights Act of 1964, signed by President Lyndon B. Johnson, prohibits discrimination of all kinds based on race, color, religion, or national origin. It outlawed discrimination in public facilities and abolished the "Jim Crow" laws in the South. Under this act, it became illegal to compel segregation of the races in schools or housing. Title I of the act barred the unequal application of voter registration requirements but did not abolish literacy tests as a prerequisite to voter registration. In 1965 Congress passed the Voting Rights Act of 1965, which declared as illegal literacy tests, poll taxes, and other voter registration requirements.

4. The "four little angels dead" (p. 98) to which *The Secret Life of Bees* refers are the four young black girls killed in the bombing of the Sixteenth Street Baptist Church in Birmingham, Alabama, on September 15, 1963. Robert Chambliss, a member of the Ku Klux Klan, was arrested and charged with murder but was found "not guilty" on October 8. He was retried with new evidence in November of 1977, found guilty, and sentenced to life in prison. He died in an Alabama prison in 1985. In 2000, the FBI announced that the bombing was perpetrated by a splinter group of the KKK, the Cahaba Boys. Two other members of this group were later tried and convicted.

5. The book references "three civil rights workers" (p. 166) killed in Mississippi. On June 21, 1964, one black and two white civil rights workers were murdered in Mississippi. They had been working to register black voters in Mississippi, were arrested by police on false charges, and jailed for several hours. They were then turned over to members of the Ku Klux Klan, who beat and murdered them. The FBI arrested several members of the Klan, but none were convicted of murder at that time. In 2005, Edgar Ray Killen was charged and convicted on three counts of manslaughter. The 1988 movie *Mississippi Burning* depicts this incident.

6. The Wailing Wall (Western Wall) is a retaining wall in Jerusalem where the Jewish people pray both night and day. Traditionally, they deposit slips of paper with their wishes and prayers on them into cracks in the wall. May's "wall" fulfills a similar need for her.

7. Depression is a serious mental disorder characterized by long periods of sadness and/or other negative feelings. A depressed person may feel guilty, helpless, or fearful and will often experience extended periods of crying. Both May Boatwright and Deborah Owens exhibit symptoms of depression.

8. A person suffering from obsessive-compulsive disorder feels burdened by unwanted thoughts and urges and may exhibit unreasonable repetition of an everyday routine. May's need to select a "perfect" banana points to this disorder.

# Initiating Activities

1. Arrange for a beekeeper to come to class and discuss his/her profession with students.

2. Discuss with students the title's possible meanings and the cover illustration. Then read aloud the synopsis and some of the blurbs on the inside front pages and back cover. Have students volunteer predictions about the book.

3. Have students research the Wailing Wall and write/present a report about places with similar significance in other cultures.

4. Have students research the Emmett Till Unsolved Civil Rights Crime Act and present its purpose and cause of creation. In addition, students should give examples of "cold cases" that the Act is meant to solve.

5. Place the following quote on an overhead transparency: "Hope deferred makes the heart sick, but when longing is fulfilled, it is a tree of life" (*Bible*, Proverbs 13:12). Brainstorm with students about "hopes" they have had delayed and how this makes them feel. Point out that the narrator of the novel, Lily, has unsuccessfully hoped for and tried to get her father's love for ten years. Brainstorm with students about how this makes Lily feel and how her quest for love and acceptance will end.

6. Have students begin a prediction chart (see page 33 of this guide) to use as they read the book.

# Chapter 1

Bees swarming in Lily's room cause her to reflect on her mother's death. Though Rosaleen loves her unconditionally, Lily struggles with emotional rejection at school and her father's cruel punishment and neglect. Rosaleen plans to register to vote but is arrested following a racially charged altercation.

| Vocabulary |
| --- |
| presumptuous |
| paradise |
| insomniac |
| conjure |
| imbecile |
| philosophy |
| oblivious |
| motes |
| parsonage |

## Discussion Questions

1. Examine the epigraph at the beginning of the chapter, and explain how you think it relates to the story. Do this for all subsequent chapters. *(Answers will vary. When Lily was four years old, her mother, i.e., the "Queen Bee" of the home, died. Lily has keenly felt the effects of her absence for the last ten years, and her lack of a mother has affected her self-image, her relationship with her peers, and her overall view of life.)*

2. Correlate the arrival of the bees with the summer of 1964 in Lily's life. Examine the allusion to the angel Gabriel and the possible implications of Rosaleen's comment that "Bees swarm before death" (p. 2). *(Lily believes the bees were sent to prepare her for the upheaval in her life during that summer. She compares their arrival to the angel Gabriel appearing to the Virgin Mary. Gabriel's arrival prepared Mary for the birth of the Christ child [Bible, Luke 1:26–35]. Just as Gabriel brought news of Mary's miraculous future, so too do the bees bring news of Lily's miraculous future. Answers will vary, but Rosaleen's comment suggests that the bees are also an ominous sign. Students should discuss various kinds of "death" that the bees may foreshadow as well as how the bees may be symbolic of both life and death.)*

3. Identify Lily's father, and discuss her relationship with him. Assess the effect this relationship has on Lily. Note the impact Mrs. Henry has on Lily's self-esteem. *(Her father, T. Ray Owens, is a peach farmer who cares only for his dog. Lily has almost no good memories of him. She repeatedly tries to connect with him to no avail. One example would be the incident where Lily wakes him to show him the bees, which have retreated into the walls. T. Ray responds as he usually does to any perceived infraction of hers—by threatening to make her kneel on grits for an extended period. T. Ray refuses to take Lily to any school events and will not buy suitable clothes for her. He also makes fun of her for reading and will not allow her to read while she is waiting to sell peaches. Answers will vary, but T. Ray's rejection and her lack of a mother cause Lily to have low self-esteem and no real sense of self-identity. In the "darkness" of her poor self-image, Mrs. Henry, her English teacher, offers Lily hope for a brighter future by telling her she is intelligent enough to become a professor or a writer. When Lily realizes T. Ray does not and will never love her, she resolves to run away.)*

4. Examine information about the death of Lily's mother, and analyze its effect on Lily. Discuss T. Ray's account of the death, and tell whether you think Lily is responsible. *(Lily's only memory of her mother is the day she died. She remembers a number of details about her mother, such as how her hair looked and how she smelled, but she can never form a clear picture of her face. She remembers her mother picking her up and dropping things into an open suitcase on the floor. This was followed by a heated argument between her parents. Her mother tried to protect her when Lily was shoved by her father. Then her mother went into the closet and grabbed a gun, which T. Ray snatched from her and began waving in the air. The next thing Lily recalls is picking up the gun off the floor and hearing it discharge. At times she thinks she was holding the gun when it exploded, but sometimes she thinks the explosion came later. The night before she started first*

*grade, T. Ray told her that her mother had been cleaning out the closet, that Lily picked the gun up off the floor, and that the gun went off and killed her mother. Lily has borne the burden of guilt for her mother's death ever since she was a small child. Answers will vary, but T. Ray was very shaken up when Lily told him what she remembers about her mother's death. This seems to imply that Lily may not be guilty after all.)*

5. Discuss the relationship between Lily and Rosaleen. *(Rosaleen is the black woman who has taken care of Lily for the past ten years. Although she has no interest in helping Lily learn to dress correctly or become more "charming," Lily knows Rosaleen loves her unconditionally and will stand up to T. Ray for her. When her father ignores her birthday, Rosaleen bakes her a cake. Lily daydreams that Rosaleen is white and becomes her real mother by marrying T. Ray or that she is a black orphan whom Rosaleen adopts. Rosaleen is appalled by T. Ray's cruel treatment of Lily, e.g., welts and bruises on Lily's knees from being forced to kneel on the grits for an hour.)*

6. Analyze how Lily reacts to life without her mother and how she copes. Note the significance of the items in the tin box. *(She misses her when faced with issues such as training bras and her desire to participate in cheerleader tryouts. She yearns for her when she has her first menstrual period because she has no one but Rosaleen with whom to share the experience. She accidentally finds a paper bag with a few traces of her mother, i.e., her picture, a pair of gloves, and a small wooden picture of a black Virgin Mary. These mementoes become Lily's "lifeline" to her mother. She keeps them in a tin box, which she buries in the orchard. Occasionally, she digs up the box and lies under the trees, wearing the gloves and smiling at her mother's photograph. She studies the caption on the back of the Mary picture, "Tiburon, S.C.," and locates the town on a map, determined to go there someday. This becomes important to the plot when she and Rosaleen run away to Tiburon.)*

7. Discuss the Civil Rights Act of 1964 (see Background Information on page 5 in this guide), and analyze its effect on Rosaleen. Note Lily's premonition. *(After watching President Johnson sign the Civil Rights Act on TV, Rosaleen resolves to register to vote and begins practicing her signature in order to pass the literacy test. Lily is worried because she overhears people at church speaking skeptically about Negroes getting their civil rights and she is aware that Martin Luther King was arrested for trying to eat in a "white" restaurant. She realizes that white people will not quietly accept the changes the Civil Rights Act is setting in motion.)*

8. Examine the cause/effect of events surrounding Lily's birthday. Analyze what this reveals about Lily and about T. Ray. *(Although T. Ray has never paid attention to her birthday, Lily hopes this year will be different; she mentions her birthday and hints at her desire for a charm bracelet. T. Ray ignores her; his silence reminds her that she doesn't even "exist" to him. Seeking consolation, Lily goes to the orchard and digs up the mementoes of her mother; she falls asleep holding them. T. Ray finds her in the orchard and thinks she has been there with a boy; he forces her to kneel on grits for an hour. Lily has hidden the pictures of her mother and Mary inside her waistband; she feels the pictures while kneeling on the grits, and it seems her mother is there with her. Lily desperately wants to be out of the house on her birthday; she goes to town with Rosaleen, which sets in motion all subsequent events in the story. Answers will vary, but Lily is bound to her life with T. Ray until she realizes that there is no love to unite them as family. T. Ray drives Lily away with his behavior. In many ways, Lily's literal and figurative journeys in the story are as much about her relationship with her father as they are about her mother.)*

9. Examine the evidence of racism toward Rosaleen, and correlate with actual events following the signing of the Civil Rights Act of 1964 (see Background Information on page 5 in this guide). *(When Rosaleen and Lily go inside the white church to rest, the minister is anxious for*

*them to leave and will not loan them fans. Three men taunt Rosaleen and call her derogatory names. She pours the spit from her snuff jug across the men's shoes. They grab Rosaleen and demand that she clean their shoes. Although the men assault her, the white police officer arrests her on charges of assault, theft [the fans], and disturbing the peace. He takes her and Lily to jail. Like the three civil rights workers killed in Mississippi, Rosaleen is arrested on false charges and beaten. Both incidents are motivated by a desire to prevent African Americans from voting.)*

10. Analyze the irony of the statement, "We loved them in the Lord, Brother Gerald said, but they had their own places" (p. 30). *(Although the minister claims to love black people, they are not welcome in his church and are not allowed to use his fans. Deliberately alienating a population of people because of their race is the very opposite of love. The minister is a hypocrite.)*

11. **Prediction:** What will happen to Rosaleen and Lily?

## Supplementary Activities

1. Mrs. Henry improves Lily's self-image and helps her see her true potential. Write a paragraph about a teacher who has been a positive influence in your life.

2. Use the Metaphors and Similes chart on page 34 of this guide to write at least one simile and one metaphor from this section. Include an interpretation for each example. This is an ongoing assignment for each section and will include both similes and metaphors where applicable. Examples: **Similes**—"wings shining like bits of chrome" (p. 1); "shadows moved like spatter paint" (p. 4); **Metaphors**—hair: tower of beauty (p. 3); Lily and Rosaleen: prize float (p. 32).

# Chapters 2–3

Lily rescues Rosaleen from the hospital where she is taken after being beaten in jail. They leave Sylvan to escape T. Ray and Rosaleen's probable death at the hands of the racists. They head for Tiburon, the town listed on the back of the picture of the black Virgin Mary. There Lily spots jars of honey bearing the same image of Mary and finds out that they are the product of a local beekeeper named August Boatwright.

| Vocabulary |
| --- |
| decapitate |
| brazen |
| wrench |
| pious |
| blaspheme |
| anointed |

## Discussion Questions

1. Discuss Rosaleen's treatment during and after her arrest. Why do you think Gaston does not protect her? *(The three men follow the police car and harass Rosaleen, but Gaston does nothing to stop them. He smiles and tells Lily that he can't predict what the men will do. When they reach the police station, the men are waiting and begin to beat Rosaleen, whose hands are handcuffed behind her back. Gaston finally intervenes, but his statement, "Now's not the time" [p. 36], implies that he will allow the men to continue the beating later. When Lily sets out to rescue Rosaleen from jail, she finds that Rosaleen is in the hospital with several stitches in her head, the result of a severe beating. Lily knows the men will eventually kill Rosaleen if she does not get her away from Sylvan. Gaston does not protect Rosaleen because he shares the racist views of her attackers.)*

2. Examine Lily's confrontation with T. Ray. Describe and analyze her reaction to his allegation that her mother left her. *(He is furious with her for being involved in Rosaleen's arrest, and Lily knows she will face a "torture chamber" of grits. Before he leaves to pay his workers, he threatens*

*her, and she stands up to him. He becomes enraged when she mentions her mother, and he tells her that her mother left her because she did not care about her. Answers will vary. While waiting for him to return, she goes through stages of rejection, despair, and rationalization. Thoughts of her mother leaving her trigger memories and tears, but she remembers that T. Ray once told her that her rabbit died to punish her. She decides that T. Ray just made up the story of her mother's rejection to punish her.)*

3. Analyze the symbolism of Lily's epiphany, "Lily Melissa Owens, your jar is open" (p. 41), and its effect on her. Examine her mixed reactions to leaving home, and note the rationale for her destination. *(Answers will vary, but like the bees in the jar, it has taken her a little while to realize that she is free because she has been conditioned to think of herself as a captive. In the moment that she hears the inner voice, she realizes that she has an opportunity to take back her life. Although she knows she must leave, she feels a tinge of sadness when she wonders if she will ever see her room again. She decides that she and Rosaleen will go to Tiburon, South Carolina, because this is the place written on the back of her mother's picture of the black Mary.)*

4. Discuss Lily's loyalty to Rosaleen, including her ingenuity in helping her escape and her concern for her afterwards. *(She tries to keep Brother Gerald from pressing charges against Rosaleen for stealing the fans by implying that Rosaleen has a hearing problem and misunderstood what he said. She lies about the reason Rosaleen poured spit on the men's shoes, telling him it was because they blasphemed Jesus. When she finds Rosaleen injured in the hospital, she devises a way to help her escape by tricking the nurses and police officer on duty. After reaching Tiburon, she steals snuff because she thinks Rosaleen deserves to have it. Throughout their ordeal, Lily is more concerned about Rosaleen's welfare than her own.)*

5. Discuss Lily's verbal confrontation with Rosaleen and their reconciliation. Analyze what this reveals about each of them. *(After Lily tells Rosaleen what T. Ray said about her mother leaving, Rosaleen accuses Lily of running away to get away from T. Ray rather than to save her. Rosaleen believes Lily is treating her like a pet dog who is supposed to follow her. She feels that Lily is acting like she is Rosaleen's "keeper" and that Lily thinks she is dumb. Lily retaliates by telling Rosaleen she is not being fair and that she is dumb because she poured snuff juice on the shoes of white men and would not apologize. Lily leaves Rosaleen alone and tells her to find her own way, but she panics when she cannot find her later and feels the same grief she feels each Mother's Day. When she finds Rosaleen, each apologizes to the other. Answers will vary, but this scene shows the effect of the cruelty and racism the two have encountered. They lash out at each other because neither one can confront the person or persons responsible for their mistreatment and anxiety.)*

6. Analyze the role of "fate" in Rosaleen and Lily's journey to Tiburon. *(A black man stops to give them a ride to within three miles of Tiburon. While browsing through the general store in Tiburon, Lily discovers a picture of a black Mary identical to the one her mother had, this time on the label of a jar of honey. The beekeeper, August Boatwright, is a black lady who lives just outside Tiburon.)*

7. Read the opening paragraph of Thoreau's *Walden*, and explain how it relates to Lily's search for peace. *(Answers will vary. Thoreau went to the woods searching for the meaning of life and to discover how to live essentially and deeply. The day after she runs away, Lily awakes amidst nature and declares this day to be the first day of her new life. Like Thoreau, she is on a quest to understand herself and the world around her. More specifically, she is searching for resolution of her guilt over her mother's death and emotional healing. She is searching for a "mother" who will give meaning to her life and teach her how to live.)*

8. Analyze Lily's naivete versus reality in regard to civil rights. *(She assumes that, since the Civil Rights Act has been signed, she and Rosaleen will find a motel or rented room in which to stay and that they can eat in restaurants if they choose. Rosaleen knows the truth, i.e., that people will have to be forced to abide by the ruling.)*

9. Correlate the epigraph at the beginning of the two chapters in this section with events. *(Answers will vary. Chapter Two: Lily is the "scout" bee who is searching for a suitable place for her and Rosaleen to start a new life. Chapter Three: Lily must first locate the place with a "circle of attendants," i.e., the Boatwright sisters, and then she can find the new queen, i.e., a substitute mother. Finding the picture of the Madonna on the honey label symbolically tells her she is headed in the right direction.)*

10. **Prediction:** How will August Boatwright react to Lily and Rosaleen's arrival?

## Supplementary Activities

1. Working in a small group, research and present an oral report on incidents of racial strife in the year preceding and following the signing of the Civil Rights Act of 1964.

2. Write a metaphor poem about rejection based on Lily's emotions after her father says her mother deserted her.

3. Continue to add to your Metaphors and Similes chart. **Similes**—"ears like little dried apricots" (p. 34); "(T. Ray's) head plowed forward like a bull wanting to gore something" (p. 42); **Metaphor**—pyramids of grits: torture chamber of food staples (p. 37)

# Chapters 4–5

After reaching Tiburon, Lily and Rosaleen find refuge and work in the home of August Boatwright and her sisters. Lily invents a tale to explain why they are in Tiburon. The Boatwright sisters introduce them to their religion, which revolves around the black Virgin Mary.

### Vocabulary

pith
sixth sense
corrugated
paranoid
meander
consolation
ambrosia
naive
bona fide
vigilante groups
orthodox
eclectic

## Discussion Questions

1. Discuss Lily and Rosaleen's arrival at the Boatwright home, and compare/contrast their reactions. (*They first see August working with her bees and looking like an "African bride." Both Lily and Rosaleen are temporarily mute—Lily because of the sight of August and Rosaleen because her mouth is sealed with snuff. Lily realizes August is the woman who makes the Black Madonna Honey and believes she has found a key to her mother's past. Lily feels they have come to the right place; Rosaleen is skeptical and wonders what they are doing there. June and May Boatwright respond to Lily's knock on the door and think they have come to buy honey. Lily interrupts Rosaleen when she tries to explain about the picture of the black Madonna and later cautions her not to say anything about the picture or about Lily's mother. Lily is not yet ready to talk to August about her background. She is enjoying the peaceful refuge of the Boatwright home and wants time to win August over so she will not be sent back to Sylvan.*)

2. Examine information about the Black Madonna statue, and analyze Lily's reaction. (*Lily sees the carving of a woman in the corner of the Boatwrights' parlor. The statue is nearly three feet tall and is totally black. Her right arm is raised, and her fingers are closed in a fist. The statue is not dressed like the Madonna on the honey label, but Lily realizes that this is the figure in the picture. She feels drawn to the statue and believes the black Mary knows all about her but still accepts her. Answers will vary, but this scene reveals Lily's self-analysis: a lying, murdering, hateful person who hates herself for killing her mother. However, the statue also gives her hope that she has inner goodness and beauty. The statue causes Lily both to love and hate herself.*)

3. Discuss the Boatwright women and the correlation between them and the epigraph's depiction of a bee colony. (*Answers will vary. The honey-loving Boatwright women comprise a "colony." August is the matriarch, i.e., the queen bee; June and May provide the support base. June teaches at the high school for black students and plays the cello for dying people in their homes and at the hospital. May does the cooking and housework.*)

4. Discuss Lily's explanation of her and Rosaleen's arrival in Tiburon, and analyze the Boatwrights' individual reactions. (*Her explanation mixes a little truth and many lies. She tells the truth when she says that her mother died when she was little and that Rosaleen was their housekeeper. On the other hand, what Lily says about their last names, the way Rosaleen incurred her injuries, her father's death in a tractor accident the month before, the authorities' plan to send her to a home, her plan to find her Aunt Bernie in Virginia, and the need for money for the trip are lies. August knows she is lying from the start, and May knows that Rosaleen has been beaten. June confronts August about Lily's lies and the need to alert the authorities about the "runaway girl." June resents Lily because she is white and does not believe that they owe her anything. August wants to give Lily time to confide in them and believes they can help her.*)

5. Examine how Rosaleen and Lily adapt to life in the Boatwright home. (*Lily feels as if she belongs with the Boatwrights [though she resents June's hostile attitude], but living with them makes her self-conscious about her whiteness and causes her to recognize her own prejudice.*)

*Her interaction with August begins to dispel her feeling that colored women are not as smart as white women. Lily hopes that things will stay just as they are, i.e., no T. Ray or people who want to hurt Rosaleen. Rosaleen is content with their new living arrangements but cannot understand Lily's reluctance to tell anyone about her mother and the picture of the black Mary. Lily and Rosaleen easily adapt to their assigned work. Lily thrives under August's training and praise and becomes quite adept at each phase of honey production. May and Rosaleen form an instant friendship and enjoy working together in the kitchen.)*

6. Discuss May's traits, and analyze the symbolism of her wall. Consider the mental illnesses described in the Background Information, and discuss May's mental state. *(Answers will vary. May is fairly stable unless someone brings up an unpleasant subject, and then she begins to hum "Oh! Susanna" to keep from crying. If the news is especially bad, she begins to cry uncontrollably [symptomatic of depression], and her sisters send her to the wall. When her reaction is unusually intense, they put her in a tub of warm water and comfort her. May cannot stand the thought of anything suffering, even a rat or an insect, and she must select a "perfect" banana every morning [symptomatic of obsessive-compulsive behavior]. August explains to Lily that April was May's twin sister and that they grew up with a strong attachment to each other. May's problems started when April became depressed over racial injustice and committed suicide. Her death caused something in May to die, too. After April's death, the entire world became "May's twin." She empathetically internalizes all the problems of the world, and in her stone wall, patterned after the Jews' Wailing Wall in Jerusalem [see Background Information], she places bits of paper on which she has written her feelings and concerns. In this way she mourns and hands her worries over to God. The wall is her defense against all of the pain in the world.)*

7. Analyze the analogy comparing Lily's life to a boxing match. *(To Lily, life has been a "boxing match" in which she has fought for survival against T. Ray and her peers' rejection. The first week at August's symbolizes a time-out when she can go to her "corner" and have her wounds treated.)*

8. Analyze the metaphor, "honey was the ambrosia of the gods and the shampoo of the goddesses" (p. 84). *(Honey is the lifeblood of the Boatwright household. It is used for everything. They swallow a spoonful to wake up in the morning and another to put them to sleep at night. It is used to calm their minds, give them stamina, and prevent infection or fatal disease. They use it in their baths, as a skin cream, and as a condiment. Honey causes Lily to gain weight and her hair to become silken and wavy.)*

9. Examine the Boatwright sisters' religion and its effect on Lily. *(Each evening the sisters kneel before the statue of the black Mary, which May calls "Our Lady of Chains," and say their rosary prayers. Lily joins them. Rosaleen sits on a chair and at first resists the prayers but eventually joins them. August explains that their religion is based on their mother's Catholicism and a mixture of their "own ingredients." August tells Lily that, if she will ask Mary's help, she will give it. She then relates a story about the nun Beatrix and how Mary "stood in" for her when Beatrix needed her most. Lily believes that August is referring to her through Beatrix. She thinks that August wants her to ask Mary for help so that she can go home. This prompts Lily to ask Mary to hide her in the Boatwrights' home so that she will never have to return to her father.)*

10. Discuss August's beekeeping business and how Lily reacts to this. Note the metaphor comparing the world to a bee yard (p. 92). *(August gives Lily a lesson in "bee yard etiquette" and tells her that the world is really one big bee yard and the same rules apply in both places: don't be afraid, but don't be an idiot; act not out of anger but out of love. After telling Lily how to behave around the bees, August has her put on bee-tending clothing and takes her on bee patrol. August explains the importance of bees remaining with their hive, and Lily decides she will make August love her enough to keep her forever.)*

11. Analyze Lily's statement, "My chest hurt from feeling things" (p. 98), and note her solution. *(She is unable to go to sleep and begins to wonder if T. Ray is concerned about her and if he realizes how badly he treated her, even though she actually believes he is thinking up ways to kill her. An intense yearning for her mother consumes her. She pictures herself climbing into bed with her mother and putting her hand on her heart as they exchange loving words. Rosaleen interrupts her "dream" world and tells her she must accept her mother's death because she is not coming back. Lily replies that she can feel her mother at the Boatwrights' and knows she has been there. Rosaleen, who is not sure whether Lily's mother left her, implies that Lily might find out something she does not want to know. As a solution to her heartache, Lily "gives" her mother to May's wailing wall by writing her name, Deborah Owens, on a piece of paper and placing it in a crevice in the wall.)*

12. **Prediction:** What will Lily learn about her mother?

## Supplementary Activities

1. Sketch one of the following: (a) the Boatwrights' house (b) one of the sisters (c) the statue of the black Mary.

2. Working in a small group, research the Wailing Wall in Jerusalem and present an oral report to the class.

3. Continue to add to your Metaphors and Similes chart. **Similes**—"(August) looked like an African bride" (p. 67); "night seemed like an inkblot" (p. 101); **Metaphors**—tops of beehives: postage stamps of white shine (p. 79); June's mouth: tight buttonhole (p. 83)

# Chapters 6–7

Lily meets June's boyfriend Neil and the Daughters of Mary. She learns the story of the wooden statue of Mary, a.k.a. Our Lady of Chains, and observes the Daughters' religious service. Lily and Zach, a black teenager employed by August, form a close working and personal relationship. June and Neil have a falling-out.

| Vocabulary |
| --- |
| ingenious |
| premises |
| solace |
| cloister |
| bordello |
| consignment |
| mites |
| deciduous |

## Discussion Questions

1. Discuss Neil, his relationship with June, and his interaction with Lily and Rosaleen. *(Neil is principal at the school where June teaches. Though he has been June's boyfriend for years, she refuses to marry him. A heated argument between Neil and June culminates in Neil accusing June of being afraid of marriage. As he is leaving, June yells at him to never come back. After Neil is introduced to Lily and Rosaleen, he asks them where they are from and how long they plan to stay. Lily provides only a couple of terse answers before leaving the house to evade further questioning.)*

2. Examine the story of "Our Lady of Chains" and its significance to the Daughters of Mary. *(August says that in the days of slavery, slaves prayed day and night for deliverance. A slave named Obadiah found the wooden figure of a black woman, with uplifted arm and clenched fist, washed up on the riverbank. He believed the statue was sent by God and took it to the slaves' praise house. An old slave named Pearl proclaimed the statue to be the mother of Jesus. The slaves believed she understood their suffering, and they painted a red heart on her breast so the people would have something to touch. Their belief in Our Lady of Chains filled them with fearlessness and defiance*

*and inspired some of them to escape. The slaves' master heard of her influence on them and repeatedly chained her in the barn, but each time she made her way back to the praise house. The slaves called her "Our Lady of Chains" because she broke her own chains and inspired them to break theirs. The story energizes the congregation, and they dance and sing. Each member of the congregation finds solace in touching the statue's fading heart. Through the connection they feel to Mary, they are relieved of their emotional bondage.)*

3. Examine the cause/effect of Lily's attempt to touch the statue. *(Just as she reaches out to touch the statue's heart, June stops the music; she is left standing with her hand outstretched. She looks at all the black faces and realizes she is not one of them; she wishes she could disappear. Lily faints; the celebration ends, May goes to the wailing wall, June goes to her room and locks the door, the Daughters huddle in the kitchen, and Lily awakens, bewildered, on August's bed. Rosaleen takes her in her arms; Lily feels unbearably sad, implying that she longs for her own mother's arms. As a result of all that has happened, Lily knows that she will return one day to touch Our Lady's heart and will then show August the picture of her mother.)*

4. Discuss Zach and his interaction with Lily. *(He is a handsome black teenager who helps August with the bees. August is his godmother, and he will be a junior at the black high school. He makes all A's and plays halfback on the football team. August has told him about Lily, but he is surprised to learn that she is white. He and Lily converse about music and his work. Lily continues to lie about why she is in Tiburon. They discuss school, and Lily opens up to him about her dream of becoming a writer and an English teacher, which now seems impossible to her. Zach confides that he wants to be a lawyer, but that, because he is a Negro, he does not feel that he has much of a future. They develop a crush on each other, but Zach cautions Lily that some people would kill boys like him for even looking at a white girl. Zach brings her a notebook to encourage her in her writing.)*

5. Discuss June's antagonism toward Lily. Brainstorm with students about why they think June dislikes Lily. *(June's aversion to Lily becomes obvious when she stops the music just as Lily is about to touch the statue. August scolds her for this, and she subsequently is polite but distant with Lily. Lily knows the politeness is just a façade but cannot understand why June resents her. Later June catches Lily in a lie about her "aunt" after mentioning that Lily and Rosaleen have been there two weeks. Answers will vary, but students should note June's earlier reference to Lily's being "white.")*

6. Analyze Lily's inner conflict over telling August the truth about why she came to Tiburon. *(As long as Lily does not tell August the truth, Lily can continue to live in her dream world and pretend that she and Rosaleen have come to stay forever with the Boatwrights. August gives her two obvious chances to tell the truth, and Lily wants to show her the black Mary picture and ask about her mother, but she does not think she can do so until she touches the statue's heart. She is afraid August will tell her she has never seen her mother, so not knowing anything at all seems better than asking and having her dream end.)*

7. Describe and analyze Lily's emotional extremes when she and Zach go to harvest the honey. Note her desire to disappear like a turtle into its shell. *(While riding with Zach, Lily feels anxious but starts to laugh when they hit a rut and their heads hit the truck roof. Her laughter becomes hysterical and for a period seems uncontrollable. When she is finally able to stop, she thinks about how nice it was to faint and how she wishes she could disappear at will like a turtle. Answers will vary, but these thoughts and her loss of emotional control seem to symbolize her desire to escape all that her life has been. When they arrive back in Tiburon, Lily erupts into hysterical crying. She at first thinks that she is crying because of fears about her future, but she realizes that she is actually crying for Zach and her intense feelings for him.)*

8. Examine the cause/effect of Rosaleen's decision to move into May's room. *(May gets scared at night by herself; Rosaleen moves into her room. Lily feels Rosaleen is abandoning her; Rosaleen assures her she will always be there for her. Lily follows Rosaleen to the house; she encounters August and realizes that August knows how lost and sad she feels [and may know who she is]. Lily is alone in the honey house; she imagines she hears Zach coming and imagines her mother calling to her.)*

9. **Prediction:** How will Lily and Zach's relationship develop?

## Supplementary Activities

1. Write a metaphor poem entitled "Infatuation" that describes Lily's feelings for Zach.

2. Working in a small group, research the first moonwalk and write a paragraph in which you support or refute the idea that this event demystified the moon and caused it to become "one more big science project" (p. 114).

3. Continue to add to your Metaphors and Similes chart. **Similes**—"(Zach) ran like the wind" (p. 117); "(bees) sound like sizzling bacon" (p. 126); **Metaphor**—the word "impossibility": big log thrown on the fires of love (p. 133)


# Chapter 8

Lily bonds closely with August but cannot bring herself to reveal the truth about her and Rosaleen's arrival in Tiburon. August tells Lily about the Boatwright sisters' background and teaches her more about beekeeping. Lily makes a collect call to her father, only to experience disappointment and rejection again. Later in the parlor by herself, Lily touches Our Lady's heart for the first time.

| Vocabulary |
| --- |
| monogram |
| siesta |
| stamen |
| sidled |
| integrate |

## Discussion Questions

1. Discuss August's explanation of the Black Madonna, and correlate with information in the Background Information section of this guide. Analyze why August puts a picture of the Black Madonna on the jars of honey and why this is important to Lily. *(August explains that hundreds of images of dark-faced Marys can be found in Europe and that the name of the one she places on her honey is the Black Madonna of Breznichar in Bohemia. August's interest in the Black Madonna began with her mother's prayer cards that featured pictures of saints, and she researched them in college. She chose to put the picture on her jars of honey to portray divinity in dark skin. The Daughters of Mary's reaction confirmed her feeling that everyone needs a God who looks like them. Although Madonna of Breznichar in Bohemia is an invented one, numerous statues or paintings of a black Virgin Mary are located in Europe, some in museums but most in churches or shrines. Answers will vary, but it seems that the image of the Black Madonna is Lily's connection to her biological mother and became her connection to the Boatwrights [particularly August, who is like a surrogate mother] when she saw the image from her mother's card on August's honey jars. Moreover, the Black Madonna is the spiritual representation of femininity and motherhood for Lily and links, to one degree or another, both of her earthly mothers.)*

2. Examine August and Lily's discourse on love and what this reveals about both of them. *(When Lily says that she loves the picture on the honey jars, August questions her about what she loves. Lily says that she loves Rosaleen and writing, and she and August discover that they both love Coca-Cola with salted peanuts and the color blue. Lily tells August of her newfound love for*

*bees and honey but holds back from saying "I love you" to August. She also wants to tell August that she loves the picture of her mother but cannot bring herself to do so. This scene is significant because it shows the mutual bond that is developing between Lily and August.)*

3. Discuss the conversation between August and Lily about the statue of Our Lady of Chains in the Boatwrights' parlor, and assess the conversation's effect on both of them. *(August tells Lily that she cannot remember exactly when her family got the statue but that it was sometime after the Civil War. It was handed down from August's grandmother to her mother and is an important part of the family history. She reveals that the statue is actually just the figurehead off an old ship, but it gave the slaves comfort and hope because they saw Mary in it. She explains that although it seems that Mary's spirit is more concentrated in some places, she is actually in everything. Answers will vary, but Lily's reaction shows that one of the key ways that she is changing during her time with the Boatwrights is that she is beginning to perceive a kind of hidden spiritual element in nature and in the machinations of everyday life. August tells Lily how her grandmother would tell the Boatwright sisters the story of Our Lady of Chains, and Lily wishes she had a story like that to live inside her and replace the story of her mother's death. In listening to August reminisce, Lily realizes that August, too, misses her mother.)*

4. Discuss August's background, and examine circumstances that have molded her into the person she now is. *(Her grandmother was a beekeeper who taught August about beekeeping. She helped August believe in the "unbelievable" [e.g., the bees singing the Christmas story on Christmas Eve] and hear silent things that no one else hears. August grew up in Richmond, the daughter of the city's first black dentist. Her mother worked in a hotel laundry and inherited little of Big Mama's spiritual sensibility although she was devout in her belief in Our Lady of Chains. August studied to become a teacher, but teaching jobs for blacks were scarce, and she worked as a housekeeper for nine years before getting her first teaching job. She fell in love once but chose not to marry because she loved her freedom more than she loved the man. Although she had a good life in Richmond, her heart was always at her grandmother's place in Tiburon. When her grandmother died, she left the property to August, June, and May. August has been keeping bees there for almost 18 years.)*

5. Analyze August's statement, "The hardest thing on earth is choosing what matters" (p. 147). Do you agree or disagree with this statement? *(August's favorite color is blue, yet she painted her house bright pink because May said the color made her feel like dancing. August chose what mattered most, her sister's happiness, over her own preference. She believes most people know what matters but do not choose it. Answers will vary.)*

6. Correlate this chapter's epigraph with the metaphor comparing the beehive to a great music box. How does the epigraph relate to Lily's own life? *(Answers will vary. The bees humming inside the hive sound like music to August's ears. As August and Lily listen to the perfect hum, i.e., thousands of bee wings fanning the air to cool down the hives, it is as though they are listening to an orchestra concert. The perfect pitch, the harmony, and the variations of volume create a music box. Inside this music box, each bee has its own role to play. The epigraph refers to the bees' need for companionship and support, and Lily realizes that this is exactly what the humming represents, i.e., they all work together to provide what is needed inside the hive. At the end of Chapter 7, Lily was feeling lonely and isolated. August forges a strong bond with her in this chapter, and Lily is rejuvenated.)*

7. Analyze the symbolism of the secret life of bees (p. 148), and note why the idea is important to Lily. *(Answers will vary. The bees' "secret" life inside the hive seems to symbolize the element of hidden spirituality in all nature. Through August, Lily has developed the ability to "hear silent things on the other side of the everyday world" [p. 144]. This ability to perceive beauty in the seemingly everyday reflects Lily's own inner beauty, and she likes that she and August have this communion of the hive's beauty. Furthermore, Lily identifies with the bees. She loves the idea of bees having a secret life because she is living her own secret life in Tiburon. No one has any idea*

*how complicated life is inside the hive, and no one [except perhaps Rosaleen] knows how complicated Lily's life is right now. Lily is drawn to the idea of the queen being the "mother of thousands" and the fact that without her, the hive will quickly deteriorate. Just as the bees need the queen, their mother, to keep them going, Lily needs a "mother" in her life. In addition, having grown up under the thumb of a patriarchal society, seeing a naturally occurring matriarchy is empowering to Lily. This hidden, naturally occurring matriarchy within the hive reflects the Boatwright sisters' own secret life independent of the constructs of a predominantly patriarchal society [as well as the sense of community that they share with other women like the Daughters of Mary]. The Boatwrights are financially successful and spiritually rich, and they have accomplished these things on their own terms, with little help or influence from the "man's world" they inhabit. As she is accepted into the Boatwrights' fold, the support that the Boatwrights' "hive" gives Lily buoys her spirit and builds her inner strength as both an independent woman and as a member of a larger community of females.)*

8. Discuss Lily's contact with the bees and how this affects her. Analyze what the black Mary's "starting to come unglued" (p. 152) symbolizes to her. *(August explains to Lily how to adapt to bees flying all around her by sending them love. As the bees cover her body, she mentally says "I love you" repeatedly and remains completely still as she mentally dances with the bees. She is momentarily part of their world, no longer an orphan but a daughter amongst countless brothers and sisters. She becomes "lost" in the bees, but when the euphoria wears off, the "motherless place" in her heart begins to ache and she relives her last memories of her mother. The bees seem to sense her pain and caress and comfort her. She associates this experience with the bees that entered her room on the peach farm, which she believes were sent to liberate her from T. Ray. Answers will vary, but the label's coming unglued may symbolize the instability of her "dream world.")*

9. Discuss evidence of racism in Tiburon. Note August's concern about Lily's going to town with Zach. *(Rumors are circulating around Tiburon that Jack Palance is coming to town and bringing a black woman with him. He plans to take her to a movie and sit with her downstairs in the white section. The town is shocked by this, and white men plan to block the entrance to the theatre. Lily goes with Zach to Clayton Forrest's office, and his white secretary is appalled when Lily tells her she is staying with the Boatwright sisters. August is reluctant to let Lily go with Zach because she realizes how volatile racial strife can be and how some people will react to a white girl being with a black boy.)*

10. Examine the cause/effect of Lily's trip to town with Zach. Note Lily's rationale for writing a letter to T. Ray, and explain why you think she tears it up. *(Zach needs to deliver honey to the lawyer's office; Lily asks to go with him. Zach and Mr. Forrest go to his office; Lily looks at the pictures on the wall. She sees a picture of Mr. Forrest and his little girl standing in the ocean; she imagines herself and T. Ray playing in the water together. Lily begins to wonder if T. Ray misses her; she calls him collect. Lily tries to explain why she left; T. Ray lashes out at her. She asks T. Ray if he knows her favorite color; he tells her he will find her and "tear [her] behind to pieces [p. 160]." Lily feels rejected; she hangs up on him. She writes a letter to T. Ray and tells him what a despicable father he is; she reads the letter and tears it up but is relieved to get the anger out of her system. Answers will vary, but students should mention that Lily is conflicted in her feelings for T. Ray.)*

11. Analyze Lily's visit and prayer to the Black Madonna. *(Alone in the parlor with the statue, Lily puts her hand over her heart and asks the Black Madonna to fix her, to help her know what to do, to forgive her, to keep "them" from finding her and Rosaleen, to help her stop lying, and to make the world better. She also asks if her mother is all right and for love from June and T. Ray. After the prayer, Lily touches the heart of the statue and claims Mary as her mother. Answers will vary, but this act may symbolize Lily's need for maternal love and guidance. Like the Daughters of Mary, Lily looks to Our Lady of Chains for solace and to free her from the bondage of her pain and struggles.)*

## Supplementary Activities

1. Write a one-page essay in which you agree or disagree with August's statement, "The hardest thing on earth is choosing what matters" (p. 147).

2. Continue to add to your Metaphors and Similes chart. **Similes**—"I could feel them (August's stories) touching me in places, like an actual shawl" (p. 146); "(Lily's words) looked like they'd been laid on the paper with branding irons (p. 161); **Metaphors**—bees: plague that freed Lily (p. 151); skin pigment: the sun, everything else in the universe: orbiting planets (pp. 154–155)

# Chapter 9

After a spirited "water battle," June finally accepts Lily. May discloses that Lily's mother had once stayed with the Boatwrights. Lily determines to tell August the truth, but her resolve crumbles when Zach is arrested because of a racist incident. May is not informed of his arrest, and upon finding out, insists on going to the wailing wall by herself.

| Vocabulary |
| --- |
| minuscule |
| nymphs |
| dander |
| oblivious |
| cunning |
| limbo |
| animation |
| catcall |

## Discussion Questions

1. Examine the cause/effect of the extreme heat on July 28. Note the metaphor, "I was seeing myself as the fire department and June as the raging inferno" (p. 169). (*The bees are suffering from the heat; August and Lily take sugar water to rescue them. Lily gets stung; August lets her know she is on her way to being a true beekeeper. May and Rosaleen frolic in the water; August and Lily join them. June angrily comes outside; Lily sprays her with water. Lily and June engage in a "water battle" [Lily as "the fire department" attempts to extinguish June's fiery rage]; Rosaleen and August tease and laugh at them. June begins to laugh and lets go of the sprinkler; Lily laughs with her and June hugs her, thus ending their hostility.*)

2. Analyze the following metaphors: (a) the mind is an elevator and (b) a "necklace of lies." Describe how each affects Lily's emotions as she rests in the honey house. (*Lily explains that every human being has a steel plate in their head, a kind of defense mechanism, through which certain secret thoughts are sometimes allowed passage. While resting on her cot, Lily finds herself unable to keep certain thoughts from entering the sliding elevator door of her mind. Although she tries to avoid thinking about her mother, "she" is the only thing that wants on Lily's "elevator." Lily feels that her dream world is unraveling around her. She finally allows herself to think about her mother and takes out her picture. She wonders what it had been like to be in her womb. Lily realizes that, although the yearning is still there, it does not consume her as much as before. The heaviness of guilt over her mother's death and the "necklace of lies" she wears constantly, i.e., all the lies she has told August to gain her acceptance, overwhelm her. She once again suppresses these thoughts and contemplates the mess people make of their lives.*)

3. Discuss how Lily discovers that her mother once stayed with the Boatwrights. Assess the effect of this discovery on Lily, and tell what you think is implied by May's going to the wall after mentioning Deborah Fontanel. (*May is sitting on the kitchen floor spreading a "highway" of broken graham crackers and marshmallow bits to lead roaches out of the kitchen. Lily remembers that her mother did the same thing, and Lily wonders if her mother learned the trick from May. When Lily asks May if she knew Deborah Fontanel, May tells her that she was the sweetest thing and once stayed in the honey house. Answers will vary, but later Lily has a nightmare in which she sees her mother, smiling and pretty but with roach legs protruding.*)

*Lily feels close to the truth but fears that what she will learn about her mother will make her an unlovable, indestructible memory. Lily becomes jittery, cannot eat, and walks around the house trying to picture her mother there. She is determined to talk to August as soon as she has the opportunity. Answers will vary, but May's humming of "Oh! Susanna" and her retreat to the wall hint at some hurtful memory connected to Deborah.)*

4. Examine the cause/effect of Lily's trip to town with Zach. Brainstorm about the importance of the phrase, "If only that had happened…" (p. 176). *(Zach is going to town to buy a part for the honey wagon; Lily goes with him. This is the day Jack Palance is rumored to be taking a black woman to the theatre; white men are standing by the ticket booth. Three black teenage boys are standing on the sidewalk looking at them; the white men taunt them. The boys ask Zach about Lily; the white men watch Zach and Lily. Jackson, one of the boys, yells out an insult; one of the white men challenges him. Jackson throws a bottle and hits the man; the white men demand to know who threw the bottle. No one, including Zach, will reveal the perpetrator; all four boys are arrested. The judge is out of town; Zach cannot be released on bail for several days. June reflects on how much May loves Zach; they decide not to tell her about the arrest. Answers will vary.)*

5. Discuss Lily and August's visit to Zach. What does Lily promise Zach? Why might Zach want her to do this? *(They are allowed to see Zach but are not allowed to be alone with him. August talks to Zach about the beehives, implying that she will not rest until he is back home and working for her. Lily senses that the wounded places inside of him are similar to her own. She promises to write down for him everything that has happened to him and realizes how important her caring enough to do this means to him. Answers will vary, but as a writer, Lily has a special kind of insight into humanity. This experience has likely been demoralizing and disillusioning for Zach. There is power in the written word, and he may be seeking vindication or simply closure. He knows that Lily will depict him and his situation with the dignity the system has denied him. If Lily finds meaning in Zach's situation, and especially if that meaning is conveyed to others, then his suffering is not for naught.)*

6. Assess May's reaction when she learns Zach is in jail, paying attention to how her reaction this time differs from other times. *(May learns about Zach's arrest in a phone call from his mother. She is unusually calm, and the others realize she has withdrawn into an unreachable place inside herself. No one has ever seen her like this. August bathes May's face, and she seems to return to reality. However, her voice is monotone and she insists on going out to the wall by herself, even though it is getting dark.)*

7. **Prediction:** What will happen to May?

## Supplementary Activities

1. Write a one-paragraph response in which you agree or disagree with August's supposition that you can be bad at something, but if you love doing it, that will be enough.

2. Write Lily's first paragraph in her story about Zach's arrest.

3. Continue to add to your Metaphors and Similes chart. **Similes**—"I sat in the truck like I had frozen" (p. 180); "swarm hanging there like a black balloon" (p. 184); **Metaphors**—August: red heart on Mary's chest, Rosaleen: Mary's fist (p. 182)

# Chapter 10

May's suicide devastates the Boatwright sisters and everyone associated with them. A vigil and funeral follow, and Lily feels accepted by the Daughters of Mary. Zach, distrustful and disillusioned, is released from jail and blames himself for May's death. May's suicide note inspires in June a renewed appreciation of Neil.

| Vocabulary |
| --- |
| loping |
| induction |
| catacombs |
| taffeta |

## Discussion Questions

1. Describe the reactions of August, June, Rosaleen, and Lily to May's death. (*Lily especially notices her hands, "little ragged cups," and the memory stays with her forever. She begins to shiver and visualize how May must have died. She becomes nauseated and vomits. Rosaleen does not make a sound but shakes uncontrollably. After they return to the house, Rosaleen and Lily sob together. Rosaleen insists that Lily sleep in the room with her, and Rosaleen sleeps in May's bed. Lily recalls the looks of love and anguish she had seen in May's face and realizes that her intense empathy had finally proven too much for her. August and June display heartbroken acceptance because, without even realizing it, they had been waiting half their lives for this to happen. May's death reminds June of April's death. August finally emits a piercing scream and drops her head on May's chest.*)

2. Examine evidence of Mr. Hazelwurst's racial prejudice in his investigation of May's death. (*He quizzes Lily extensively about her status as an orphan and her living situation and asks her if she was the girl who visited Zach at the jail. His main hangup in believing Lily's story does not even seem to be its overly long and circuitous nature. Rather, he simply cannot comprehend that a white girl would willingly stay with a family of black people. He advises her to call her aunt and ask her to come right away because she is lowering herself by staying with black people. He does not seem to realize that this situation is not about her and Rosaleen but about May's death.*)

3. Discuss the vigil for May and its effect on those involved. Note Lily's request for "a sign," and explain what you think is the significance of throwing seeds into May's grave. (*August explains to Lily that sitting with May until she is buried will help them accept her death and will help May's spirit ascend to God quickly because they are telling her it is all right. As they place May's body in front of Our Lady of Chains, June plays "Oh! Susanna" while August, Rosaleen, and Lily stand beside the coffin. Lily takes May's hand and mentally tells her that she hopes she will be happier in heaven. She also asks May to look up her [Lily's] mother and ask her to send her a sign that she loves her. Zach arrives with Clayton, and the Daughters of Mary bring heaps of food. They all eat a mixture of seeds as a means of keeping them from despair. They joke and laugh about the white people's drive-by funeral home, and Lily feels that she is truly a part of the group. The vigil continues for four days. Answers will vary, but it is reasonable to say that everyone throws seeds into May's grave because seeds are a symbol of life. For May, it is a symbol of her new life in heaven, and for those in attendance, it is a symbol of their determination to continue living.*)

4. Assess the effects of jail and May's death on Zach. How does August attempt to console him? (*He assures everyone he is fine, but Lily realizes he has changed. With tears pouring down his face, he tells them he is sorry. He feels May's death is his fault because if he had told the police officer who threw the bottle, he would not have been put in jail and May would not have died. August assures him that it is not his fault and points out that if she had told May from the beginning about his arrest or had stopped her from going to the wall that night, none of this would have happened. She concludes by telling him it was May who did it. Lily is afraid he will continue to blame himself, however, just as she still blames herself for her mother's death.*)

5. Examine the significance of "draping the hives" and how this affects Lily. *(August, Lily, and Zach drape a square of black crepe material over each hive, leaving the bees' entrance open. Doing so deters the bees from leaving. August explains that it is said that a person's soul will be reborn into the next life if bees are around. Draping the hives reminds the living that "life gives way into death, and then death turns around and gives way into life" [p. 206]. This discourse makes Lily wish she could lie down in a beehive tomb like the Greeks and be reborn. To Lily, bees buzzing around just before May's burial are symbolic of May's soul having flown away.)*

6. Analyze May's suicide note and its effect on her sisters. *(August finds the note close to where May died. In the note, May expresses sorrow at leaving in this way and making her sisters sad but reminds them how happy she will be with April and others in their family who have died. She is tired of carrying around the weight of the world and must have relief. She emphasizes that it is her time to die and their time to live; she then cautions them not to "mess it up." August and June cling to each other and discuss whether it was really May's time to die. August declares that May's desire for them "to live" includes June's letting go of her fear of being jilted and marrying Neil. June becomes so attentive to Neil that everyone notices it.)*

7. Discuss the parallel between the grieving process and August's concern that, if the hives are covered too long, the bees might not find their way home again. *(Answers will vary. August understands the need to let go of grief and begin to live again. If mourning continues too long, it becomes a way of life and people may never find their way back to happiness and peace. Lily, who has been grieving for her mother for ten years, knows how hard it is to let go and really live.)*

8. Compare/contrast May's life with the epigraph at the beginning of the chapter. *(Answers will vary. After April's death, May lost much of her joy in living and became primarily a "worker bee" whose life revolved around her work in the kitchen and her trips to the wailing wall. Others' troubles consumed her and ultimately caused her death, just as the dangers that worker bees face in their foraging trips often kill them early in life.)*

## Supplementary Activities
1. Working in a small group, research and prepare an oral report on depression: causes, symptoms, treatment. Correlate your findings with May's signs of depression.

2. Continue to add to your Metaphors and Similes chart. **Similes**—"words streaming behind us like ribbons in the night" (p. 191); "wind rose up...like an oven blast, like the sudden breezes of hell" (p. 192); **Metaphor**—love and anguish: blaze that burned May up (p. 199)

# Chapters 11–12
After a week of mourning, the Boatwright sisters and their friends gather to celebrate Mary Day. June and Neil become engaged, and Lily and Zach's relationship deepens. August tells Lily about Deborah and her marriage to T. Ray, Lily's birth, and Deborah's nervous breakdown. Lily tells August the truth about her and Rosaleen's departure from Sylvan and about her guilt over her mother's death.

## Discussion Questions
1. Discuss the effect on Lily of her ongoing yearning for her mother. *(She is unable to have her talk with August because she and June are in mourning and Lily seldom sees her. She looks for a "sign of love" from her mother but never finds one. She studies a map and tries to decide where she and Rosaleen might go next. At times she does not feel like getting out of bed and quits caring about much of anything, signifying that she is losing hope.)*

| Vocabulary |
| --- |
| industrious |
| mull |
| sauntered |
| exorcism |
| shackled |
| neurotic |
| apiary |
| bolstered |

2. Discuss Zach and Lily's conversations. Examine how Zach's arrest changes him, and note Lily's reaction. *(Lily wonders how things would be between Zach and herself if she were black. He tells her that they cannot change their skin but must change the world. His arrest has left him with a lot of anger, and much of Zach's conversation revolves around racial strife. Lily begins to miss the peaceful Zach she once knew. Later she tells him about a time when some boys held her down and put a stringer of mostly live fish around her neck. No fish survived, and she blames herself for not saving them. When Zach tells her that he sometimes becomes so angry that he wants to kill something, she compares him to the boys who made her wear the fish because they were angry at the world. She asks him to promise her that he will not become like that. He kisses her and assures her that he will study hard during the coming year because his experience in jail has given him the determination to leave Tiburon and go to college. They express deep feelings for each other, and Zach tells her that one day, after he becomes "somebody," he will find her and they will be together.)*

3. Discuss how the end of the mourning period affects Lily and the Boatwright household. *(They begin to eat together, laugh and talk, and pray together. Lily feels content and decides that she will move back into the honey house. She regrets this decision, however, because being alone in the honey house means she is alone with her thoughts and fears. She takes both her mother's picture and the black Mary picture from her bag and is determined to talk to August as soon as she can.)*

4. What is Mary Day, and how do the Daughters of Mary celebrate this occasion? How does Lily feel about Mary Day? *("Mary Day" is what May called The Feast of the Assumption, the Roman Catholic celebration commemorating the Virgin Mary's passage into heaven, body and soul. The Daughters of Mary celebrate the day with elaborate decorations and abundant food. They honor Our Lady of Chains and give thanks for the honey crop. The Daughters stand in a circle and distribute tiny pieces of honey cake in a ritual similar to Holy Communion. Lily is moved by the ritual but thinks that the Pope would have fainted if he had witnessed it and that Brother Gerald would have wanted to perform an exorcism. They bring Our Lady of Chains into the honey house and reenact her story, chaining her up there for the night. While Lily is enthralled with the idea of Our Lady spending the night in the honey house, she cannot bear to see the statue chained because it reminds her of her own bondage, her own pain.)*

5. Analyze changes in June. *(In her suicide note, May told her sisters that it is time for them to live, and this has a monumental effect on June. She goes out with Neil every day, sitting as close to him as she can. She accepts his proposal of marriage and proudly wears her engagement ring. Her change of heart toward Lily is obvious when, after feeding the pinch of honey cake to her, she apologizes for being so hard on Lily when she first arrived.)*

6. Examine the cause/effect of Lily's "heart-to-heart" talk with August. *(Nothing is as important to Lily as knowing about her mother; she goes to August's room to wait for her. August arrives, and Lily tells her she needs to talk; Lily realizes she cannot turn back when August closes the door. Lily puts the picture of her mother on the chest; August tells Lily she looks just like the picture. Lily tells August that this is her mother; August tells her that she knows her mother is Deborah Fontanel Owens. Lily realizes August has known the truth all along; August reveals that she has known who Lily is from the beginning because she looks like her mother and because of her name. Lily tells August about the incident with May and the roaches; August begins telling her about Deborah.)*

*Lily tells August that she lied about her father being dead; she finds out August knows about T. Ray. Lily tells August about T. Ray's claim that her mother left her; August holds her while she cries. Lily tells August how and why she and Rosaleen left Sylvan; she feels self-recrimination about all the wrong things she has done. Lily "confesses" that she killed her mother and reveals her belief that she is unlovable; August tells her that, even if she accidentally killed her mother, she is a dear, lovable girl. August tells Lily that she loves her; Lily wants to respond with "I love you" but can't get the words out, revealing her struggle to give and receive love.)*

7. Explain why you think Lily is unable to tell August that she loves her. *(Answers will vary, but the harshness of Lily's upbringing and the fact that she was not well-liked in school have likely created trust issues for her. Giving and accepting love requires one to trust, to leave oneself vulnerable to the other person. Lily is still afraid of getting hurt.)*

8. Discuss what Lily learns about her mother and father. Assess how this information affects her. *(August once worked as a housekeeper for the Fontanel family and took care of Deborah. She tells Lily about Deborah's childhood and the things she loved. She reveals that she gave Deborah the picture of the black Mary shortly before she died and that Lily is much like her mother, i.e., brave enough to do something other girls would not dream of doing [like running away]. After Deborah's mother died, she moved to Sylvan, where she met Terrence Ray Owens. August says that T. Ray was not always like he is now. He loved her mother and initially treated her like a princess. Upon finding out that Deborah was pregnant with her when she married T. Ray, Lily becomes convinced that she was an unwanted baby. August, however, assures her that her mother loved her and was proud of her. Deborah was happy for a short time and tried to make the marriage work, but eventually she became disheartened and planned to leave T. Ray. When Lily learns that her mother left her with T. Ray when she went to stay with August, she is overwhelmed by feelings of rejection. She says that she hates her mother, and August tries to explain to her that her mother was depressed and this caused her to do things she ordinarily would not do. August goes on to tell Lily that Deborah did eventually return to Sylvan to get her. This revelation triggers Lily's memory of the day her mother died. She remembers her mother packing, T. Ray's arrival, the fight between them, and the gun exploding. After her talk with August, the phrase "Left you" drums repeatedly in Lily's mind. She knows that she has traded a pack of lies for a pack of truth and is unsure which is the greater burden.)*

9. Analyze the symbolism of the allusion to "Stopping by Woods on a Snowy Evening" (p. 237). *(The poem speaks of the lovely, dark, deep woods, i.e., a place of peace on the edge of civilization, away from responsibilities. Lily has found peace like this with the Boatwrights. Like the speaker in the poem, Lily wants to escape the pressures of life but knows that she has "promises to keep" and "miles to go before she sleeps." Her quest to resolve her feelings of guilt and find closure in her mother's death is not over.)*

10. Correlate the epigraph at the beginning of Chapter 12 with Lily's assessment of her mother after she learns she was an unwanted child who was deserted for three months. *(Answers will vary. Just as the queen spends her days in darkness in the hive, Deborah spent her days isolated on a farm with a husband she did not love. The queen is the "mother of the hive," yet she does not have the maternal instincts or ability to care for her young. Lily believes her mother should have been there to love and protect her but failed to fulfill that role. Even though August tries to help Lily understand that her mother made a terrible mistake and tried to fix it, Lily's feelings of abandonment persist.)*

## Supplementary Activities

1. Working with a partner, reenact the dialogue between August and Lily in which August tells Lily about her mother.

2. Continue to add to your Metaphors and Similes chart. **Similes**—"Coming into his (Zach's) presence was like stepping up to a gas heater" (p. 216); "half moon wedged like a gold coin into a slot" (p. 234); **Metaphors**— spider web: veil spun from the night (p. 229); Zach: drum major for freedom (p. 231)

# Chapters 13–14

Lily reacts to the information about her mother with a violent outburst. Rosaleen consoles her and helps clean up the mess. The Mary Day celebration concludes, and August gives Lily a hatbox full of her mother's belongings. Lily realizes that her mother did love her. Lily takes time to grieve, and Rosaleen registers to vote. T. Ray finds Lily, and she stands up to him. August convinces him to allow Lily to stay with her. Lily realizes that she has found many mothers.

| Vocabulary |
|---|
| contemptible |
| embalm |
| melancholy |
| demoralized |
| trolling |

### Discussion Questions

1. Analyze the reasons for and the effect of Lily's violent outburst. Note her empathy for Our Lady of Chains. *(Lily feels sad and disillusioned after learning her mother actually left her. She feels "chained" and has the urge to remove the chains from Our Lady. Lily tries to tell herself that what she did to her mother was worse than what her mother did to her. However, she cannot overcome her sense of abandonment. Her anger explodes and, because she wants to throw something to heaven and knock God off His throne, she picks up one of the honey jars and hurls it as hard as she can. She throws and breaks every jar, spattering honey everywhere, and then throws a bucket and a tray of candle molds at the wall. After her outburst, she feels physically sick. In this moment, Lily's dream of having a mother who loved her seems dead. She whispers, "How come you left me?" and curls up on the floor, knowing that everything, even her hatred, has drained out. Seeking refuge from the hurt, she imagines herself crawling inside the black Mary statue and hiding from the world.)*

2. Discuss what Rosaleen does for Lily and what she reveals in their conversation. *(Rosaleen takes care of Lily's wound from the broken glass and helps her clean up the mess she made. She demands to know the reason for Lily's outburst, and Lily tells her what August divulged about her mother's leaving her. Rosaleen discloses that she suspected this was true because of things she had heard. Rosaleen's heart is filled with compassion for Lily.)*

3. Analyze the symbolism of the last part of the Mary Day ceremony, and discuss Lily's reaction. *(Answers will vary. The removal of the chains seems symbolic of Mary's rising to heaven as well as the Daughters' hope for a future free of racial discrimination. Lily wants to "rise" above the pain of her mother's rejection, but she is unable to think of anything but an image of her mother leaving on a bus. The Daughters begin to bathe the statue in honey, a preservative. In this way, they are symbolically showing the everlasting nature of their inner strength. They ask Lily to join them, and as she helps them rub honey into the statue and then wash it off, she feels contentment for the first time since learning about her mother. Lily used to think of her own mother and put on her white gloves when she needed strength, but she found that she had outgrown those gloves. With her hands covered in the honey, Lily gains a new pair of golden gloves. She feels solidarity with this community of women, and she feels the power of the inner universal mother that will help her overcome her pain.)*

4. Discuss the contents of the box that August gives Lily, and examine their effect on Lily. Correlate this with Lily's wish for a sign of her mother's love (pp. 202, 215) and the miracle she would like to be hers (p. 271). *(The box contains some of her mother's belongings, including a pocket mirror, a hairbrush with one long, wavy hair in the bristles, a gold pin, a book of poetry, and a picture of Lily with her mother. Seeing her mothers' things, particularly the hair, makes Lily realize that no matter how hard she tries to forget, her mother will never disappear from her heart. Arranging the things on her bed reminds Lily of trying to organize the Christmas presents she received from her father [the same every year] into a picture of love. The picture of her smiling mother leaning toward her and feeding her enthralls Lily. This is the "sign" she has searched for, the one that lets her know that her mother loved her. The healing power of this sign eventually helps her fulfill her earlier wish to be "raised from the dead.")*

5. Analyze the metaphors in the poem: Deborah as "William Blake's rose" and Lily as one of the "invisible worms" in the "rose." *(Answers will vary. Deborah, i.e., the Rose, is sick because "invisible worms" have come in the night and destroyed her joy and ultimately her life. With the knowledge that she was an unplanned child, Lily sees herself as one of the "worms" that kept Deborah tied to T. Ray and eventually caused her death.)*

6. Analyze the simile, "It (Lily's heart) sat like an ice sculpture in the center of my chest" (p. 277), and the significance of the mouse bones she finds under her cot. *(Although Lily suffers physically from the extreme heat, her inability to forgive her mother leaves her cold emotionally. She thinks she would rather die than forgive and tries to avoid thinking about her mother by pushing the box of Deborah's things under her cot. While doing so, Lily finds the mouse bones, washes them, and carries them with her every day. Answers will vary, but they seem to represent the hurt and wounds that she harbors. When she is finally able to forgive her mother, she no longer needs to carry the bones around. Her need to "nurse" the bones is symbolic of her own healing process.)*

7. What is the "turning point" in Lily's process of acceptance/forgiveness? Tell how this changes her outlook on life, and provide examples. *(As the two Boatwright sisters prepare for June's wedding, Lily observes them embracing and talking about how much May would have loved the event. June expresses regret that she did not marry Neil while May was still alive. August, who sees Lily in the doorway, tells June, "Regrets don't help anything..." [p. 284]. Lily knows the words are also directed to her, and this marks a significant change in her attitude. She accepts her life as it is and decides that she is ready to "live." Answers will vary, but examples include: (a) being hungry and taking an interest in things around her; (b) regretting her failure to go with Rosaleen to register to vote; (c) wanting to tell Rosaleen she is proud of her; (d) calling Zach; (e) telling Rosaleen she loves her; (f) cleaning the honey house thoroughly and discarding old stuff; (g) displaying her mother's things.)*

8. Refer to the epigraph on page 277. Analyze the significance of a hive without a queen, and correlate this with Lily's growing up without a mother. *(Answers will vary. When the queen dies, the colony will also die without intervention, i.e., placing a new queen in the hive. Motherless and lonely, Lily almost "dies" emotionally, but through their love, August and her other new "mothers" help Lily to live again.)*

9. Discuss August's explanation of the significance of Our Lady of Chains (p. 288) and the effect this has on Lily. *(Lily believes it is necessary to touch the statue's heart again in order to renew her strength. August explains to her that "Our Lady" is not some magical being like a fairy godmother and she is not the statue in the parlor. Rather, Mary is something inside the heart, and Lily must find this power and strength inside herself. She tells Lily this strength has always been*

*there and is what helped her survive her father's cruelty. In addition, she says that Mary is the love inside of us and that persisting in love is the purpose of humanity. Answers will vary, but when T. Ray finds Lily and commands her to go home with him, she has the inner strength to resist him and the love to see through his anger and feel compassion for him.)*

10. Examine the cause/effect of T. Ray's arrival at the Boatwrights' home. *(T. Ray's phone bill reveals that Lily's collect phone call was made from Tiburon; Clayton Forrest's secretary tells him where to find her. T. Ray comes to the Boatwrights' intent on taking her home; he notices the pin Lily is wearing. T. Ray demands to know where Lily got the pin; she tells him that August gave it to her and that Deborah was wearing it when she came to Tiburon. T. Ray tells Lily that he looked everywhere for her mother but could not find her; Lily realizes how much her father has lost. T. Ray knocks Lily down; he loses control and believes she is Deborah. T. Ray calls her Deborah and threatens her with a knife; Lily realizes that he thinks she is his wife. Lily shouts "Daddy!"; T. Ray regains his senses and tells Lily that she looks like her mother. He says that they are going home; Lily tells T. Ray that she is not leaving. August, Rosaleen, and the Daughters arrive; T. Ray's resolve crumbles. August helps him "save face" by asking if Lily can stay; T. Ray replies, "Good riddance," and leaves.)*

11. Discuss the final question Lily asks T. Ray and his response. Do you think Lily actually caused her mother's death? *(She runs after him to ask if she really killed her mother. He replies that, although she did not mean to, Lily did cause the gun to go off. Answers will vary. T. Ray's relatively peaceful demeanor would seem to suggest that he is telling the truth. However, T. Ray has shown that he is capable of violence, and his actions around Lily when he thinks she is Deborah leave room for doubt. Lily herself says that you can never be sure that T. Ray is telling the truth.)*

12. Discuss the denouement and what it reveals about Lily. *(Lily's search is over as she turns to see all the loving women waiting for her. She still sometimes imagines a Christmas gift arriving from her father and a card signed "Love…." Lily lives in the house with August and Rosaleen, and she has discovered that forgiving her mother and herself is an ongoing process. She continues to nurture her inner strength, having become the "wall keeper" and visiting Our Lady of Chains every day. Mr. Forrest is working out the problems that Lily and Rosaleen had in Sylvan, and his daughter, Becca, becomes Lily's first real friend close to her own age. In this new friendship and her continued relationship with Zach, it is evident that Lily is opening up to others and emerging as a confident and independent young woman.)*

## Supplementary Activities

1. Sketch your impression of the "many moons" watching over Lily, or write a poem entitled "Home at Last" reflecting the end of Lily's quest.

2. Continue to add to your Metaphors and Similes chart. **Similes**—"(Lily) feeling like a concrete block" (p. 258); "smile…like sparklers going off" (p. 275); **Metaphors**—month of August: griddle (p. 277); Lily's "mothers": moons shining over her (p. 302)

# Post-reading Discussion Questions

1. Using the Character Chart on page 35 of this guide, discuss when each character experiences each emotion. *(Answers will vary. Frustration: Lily—Rosaleen refuses to apologize to the three racists; August—unable to get Zach out of jail; T. Ray—Deborah leaves Lily with him; Rosaleen—unable to register to vote when she first tries; Anger: Lily—discovers the truth about her mother's leaving her; August—June stops playing the music as Lily approaches Our Lady; T. Ray—thinks Lily is Deborah; Rosaleen—feels Lily has treated her like a "pet dog"; Fear: Lily—thinks August will reject her when she learns the truth about her; August—unable to find May; T. Ray—arrival of August and Daughters when he is threatening Lily; Rosaleen—attacked by three white men; Humiliation: Lily—forced to wear a necklace of fish; August—unable to find work as a teacher because she is black; T. Ray—must back down before August; Rosaleen—beaten because she is black; Relief: Lily—arrives in Tiburon; August—June agrees to marry Neil; T. Ray—August offers him a face-saving way to let Lily go; Rosaleen—safely escapes from the hospital; Empathy: Lily—realizes that August misses her mother; August—allows Lily to reveal the truth in her own time; T. Ray—N/A; Rosaleen—senses Lily's heartache over her mother's desertion)*

2. Use the Character Attribute Web on page 36 of this guide to analyze Lily's attributes. This will also work well for Rosaleen, Zach, the Boatwright sisters, T. Ray, or Deborah. *(Answers will vary. Acts: brave [rescues Rosaleen, adapts to bees swarming around her], nonchalant [about her father's neglect], loving [toward Rosaleen, the Boatwrights, Zach], angry [her mother's desertion, mistreatment of Rosaleen and Zach]; Says: "I hate you" to T. Ray, "I'll put it in a story" [p. 185] to Zach, "Fix me..." to the black Mary statue, "They're gonna kill you..." [p. 47] to Rosaleen; Looks: neglected [hair and clothing], much like her mother, frightened [Zach's arrest], pretty and clean [as the Mary Day celebration begins]; Feels: unloved, unwanted, lonely, sad)*

3. Use the Herringbone Chart on page 37 of this guide to examine the details of Lily's quest. *(Answers will vary. Main idea: Lily searches for acceptance, forgiveness, and a mother's love; Where: leaves Sylvan, comes to Tiburon; Does what: rescues Rosaleen from racists, runs away from her cruel father; When: summer and autumn of 1964; Who: Deborah was killed when Lily was four, leaving her with guilt and abandonment issues; T. Ray's neglect, rejection, and cruelty make her feel unloved and unwanted; August helps her find acceptance and forgiveness; How: sneaks away while her father is paying his workers, tricks a nurse and a police officer at the hospital to help Rosaleen escape, goes to Tiburon and finds love, acceptance, and several "mothers," discovers spirituality and inner strength; Why: needs to know the truth about her mother, needs to realize her own self-worth)*

4. Use the Story Map on page 38 of this guide to analyze the novel's plot development. *(Answers will vary. Setting: Sylvan and Tiburon, South Carolina, 1964; Characters: Lily Owens, T. Ray, Rosaleen, August and her sisters, Zach; Problem: Lily has unresolved guilt and needs to know the truth about her mother. Conflict: [person vs. society]—Rosaleen is attacked by racists and arrested for defending herself; Zach is arrested because he will not betray his friends who were provoked by racists; [person vs. person]—Lily is angry at and fearful of T. Ray and runs away; [person vs. self]—Lily cannot forgive herself because she thinks that she killed her mother; May struggles with grieving over the sorrows of the world. Climax: [1] Lily reacts in a violent outburst after realizing her mother did leave her because she was deeply depressed. [2] T. Ray finds Lily at the Boatwrights' home. Turning Point Incident: [1] Lily realizes regrets do not change anything. [2] She realizes her inner strength and stands up to T. Ray. Resolution: After August offers him a way to "save face," he allows Lily to stay. Lily forgives her mother and herself and finds "many mothers," i.e., Our Lady of Chains, August, and the Daughters of Mary.)*

5. Analyze the myriad of emotions Lily feels because of her mother and the effect these emotions have on her. *(Answers will vary. Love: She yearns to have a mother's love, i.e., someone to hold her when she is sad or lonely, someone to protect her from T. Ray's cruelty, someone to teach her about growing up. She continually searches for a "sign" that her mother loves her. She receives her sign when August gives her the picture showing her mother smiling at her, and she begins to believe that her mother did love her. Anger: She is angry because her mother left her with T. Ray. Rejection: When she learns that her mother did desert her for three months, she wonders how a mother could leave her child and not care what happened to her. Growing up without a mother makes her feel unwanted and unloved. Guilt: T. Ray says that she was holding the gun when it accidentally discharged and killed her mother. She blames herself but cannot remember exactly what happened. For ten years, she lives with self-recrimination and remorse. Alienation: She attributes her alienation from her peers to her mother's absence because she has no one to help her buy pretty clothes or to attend school functions with her. Loneliness: She has no close friends her own age and tries to ease her loneliness by going to the orchard to hold her mother's things and imagine what it would be like to have a mother.)*

6. Analyze the symbolism of the Black Madonna, a.k.a. Our Lady of Chains. Note August's explanation to Lily of the statue's importance. *(In the story that August tells, the statue gives the slaves hope that they can be free. To the Daughters of Mary, the ritual of wrapping the statue in chains and releasing her symbolizes the freeing of their ancestors, the hope of a future free of racial oppression, and liberation from any pain that enslaves the soul. The "sisterhood of women" built around the statue also surrounds the Daughters with love and acceptance, and Lily finds validation in being part of the group. August explains to Lily that Our Lady is neither a magical being nor just a statue in the parlor; she is something inside everyone that gives them the strength to get through life. Lily discovers that she has that strength inside her own heart.)*

7. Examine the circumstances that contributed to T. Ray Owens becoming an abusive, negligent father. How might he have been affected by Deborah's desertion? How do you think this affected his relationship with Lily? *(Answers will vary. Lily learns that her father had not always been cruel and that he did once love her mother. He and Deborah married because she was pregnant with Lily. After their marriage, Deborah became disenchanted with him, and she eventually left him and Lily. Since Deborah's death, T. Ray has only loved his dog Snout. Deborah's desertion may have left him with trust issues, and this means that he only feels comfortable showing love for another living thing if he is guaranteed unconditional love. Snout is a dog, so this is a "safe" relationship for T. Ray. Also, August commented that T. Ray "worshipped" Deborah. To have been treated with such disregard by someone he valued so highly likely left T. Ray with feelings of inadequacy. Deborah had commented that she disliked T. Ray's dirty fingernails, and T. Ray has a habit of cleaning beneath his fingernails with a knife. Through this habit, T. Ray is perpetually attempting to be good enough for Deborah. He projects his anger and frustration with Deborah onto Lily. To him, she is nothing more than a physical remnant of his relationship with Deborah. She is at his beck and call under threat of physical punishment, and he refuses to show her the love she needs, all because Deborah violated his sense of trust when she deserted him. In his relationship with Lily, it is essential for T. Ray to retain complete control, the kind of control that eluded him in his relationship with Deborah while she was alive. Like Lily, T. Ray is defined by his unresolved issues with Deborah.)*

8. Discuss the importance of the setting to the plot and to the author's main message. *(The racial strife of the 1960s is a vital component of the novel. South Carolina provides the backdrop for the intensity of racial prejudice. If the setting had been in the north, Rosaleen and Zach would not have been arrested, and much of the tension and conflict that drive the novel's action would*

*have been nonexistent. Furthermore, one of the author's main messages, that the purpose of human life is "not just to love—but to persist in love" [p. 289], would have carried much less weight. The setting enabled the author to incorporate a viable threat to love—racism—and illuminate the importance of love and the struggle to persist in it.)*

9. Analyze who best fits the role of "Queen Bee" in the novel. *(Answers will vary. Suggested answers: [1] August is the matriarch, i.e., the Queen Bee, of the Boatwright family. She is the one in whom Lily eventually confides about her guilt over her mother's death and her anger toward her mother. The other Daughters of Mary respect her as their leader, and she provides stability for all who need her. [2] The Black Madonna is the Queen Bee of the Daughters' religion, and she provides them with strength, courage, and love. [3] Lily's mother is the Queen Bee who left her "hive" and allowed her "little bee" to suffer and almost die without her.)*

10. Examine the symbolism of the moon throughout the novel. *(The Virgin Mary is often shown standing on a moon. Thus the moon can be interpreted as a symbol of Divine Mothers and feminine spirituality. Lily, in her idealization of Deborah, initially sees her as a kind of "Divine Mother." Lily is sustained throughout her difficult life by this idealization of her mother, and this is reflected in the author's depiction of the moon: "The moon was a perfect circle.... the moon was my heart beating up there in the dark" [pp. 22–23]. Shortly after Lily arrives in Tiburon, she dreams that the huge, round, perfect-looking moon cracks apart and falls from the sky. Later August comments that landing on the moon will demystify it for people and that humanity's view of it will never be the same. Both incidents foreshadow the disillusionment that Lily experiences when she finds out the truth about her mother. When Rosaleen seems to imply that Deborah left Lily, Lily's loneliness and doubt are reflected in the night sky, in which there is only starlight: "The night seemed like an inkblot I had to figure out. I...studied the darkness, trying to see...some sliver of light" [p. 101]. And though Lily finds that she can no longer rely on the perception she had of her mother for inner strength, she discovers new Divine Mothers in Our Lady of Chains, August, and the Daughters of Mary. Our Lady of Chains bears the image of a crescent moon on her breast, and Rosaleen, August, and the Daughters of Mary are referred to as "the moons shining over [Lily]" [p. 302]. These Divine Mothers are a part of Lily, omnipresent in their love and an unfailing source of inner strength.)*

11. August says that a human being's purpose is "not just to love—but to persist in love" (p. 289). Explain how the novel's characters exemplify this purpose. *(Answers will vary. Lily's entire personal journey is one of love, and one of the obstacles she must face is the truth about her mother. She manages to forgive and accept her mother, and realizes that "[her] mother...would never disappear from the tender places in [her]" [p. 273]. A challenge that Lily and June must overcome is their own prejudice. Lily has grown up thinking that black people are mentally inferior to white people, and her love and admiration of the Boatwrights inspires her to correct this fault within herself. This is evident as she begins to see ways in which she has slighted Rosaleen, as well as in her complete confidence in Zach's academic abilities. June is initially resentful of Lily's presence in the Boatwright household because she is white and because August worked as a maid for Lily's grandmother. For June, Lily at first seems to be a symbol of racial oppression, but the "water battle" allows June to see Lily for who she truly is—a playful 14-year-old girl—and June learns to love her. Other examples of characters persisting in love include: June's decision to marry Neil despite her fear of being jilted, Lily's hope that T. Ray will express love for her, August's love of Lily regardless of her lies, Zach and Lily's continued love/friendship despite society's disapproval, and May's sweetness and compassion despite her inner pain.)*

# Post-reading Extension Activities

## Writing

1. In two separate paragraphs, explain how Lily views herself and how August views her.

2. Write a diamente poem contrasting "Rejection" and "Acceptance."

3. Write a short sequel about Lily's and Zach's lives in 1975. Include other characters from the novel.

## Art

4. Create a collage depicting Lily's emotions throughout the novel.

5. Create a montage representing significant objects and places from the story.

## Listening/Speaking

6. Write a monologue in which Lily addresses her father five years after he leaves her in Tiburon.

## Current Events

7. Bring to class newspaper or magazine articles about civil rights' issues.

8. Compile articles about bees and beekeeping, and mount these on a poster board.

## Drama/Music

9. Write a ballad about May's life set to the tune of "Oh! Susanna."

10. Working in a small group, write and stage one of the scenes from the novel, e.g., Lily's rescuing Rosaleen from the hospital, the final confrontation between Lily and T. Ray, one of Lily and August's talks. Present to the class via video or live performance, adding appropriate lighting and background music.

## Research

11. Working with a partner, prepare an oral report on various artistic representations of the Virgin Mary and the stories associated with these depictions.

12. Working with a partner, research and prepare a time line for the Civil Rights movement during the 1960s. Be sure to include information about the signing of the Civil Rights Act of 1964 and Martin Luther King's "I Have a Dream" speech.

# Assessment for *The Secret Life of Bees*

Assessment is an ongoing process. The following ten items can be completed during the novel study. Once finished, the student and teacher will check the work. Points may be added to indicate the level of understanding.

Name _____ Date _____

**Student**  **Teacher**

_____  _____  1. Play the Vocabulary Card Game on page 39 of this guide.

_____  _____  2. Working with a partner, write five review questions over the novel. Combine your questions with your classmates', and participate in an oral review.

_____  _____  3. Display or present your extension project on the assigned day.

_____  _____  4. Correct all quizzes taken over the novel.

_____  _____  5. Working in a small group, stage a radio or TV interview with Lily as an adult advocate for children's rights, based on her own experiences.

_____  _____  6. Compare your completed literary analysis and comprehension charts with members of a small group.

_____  _____  7. Portray a character from the book in a game of charades.

_____  _____  8. Compare your metaphor/simile lists with a partner.

_____  _____  9. Explain to the class how one of the novel's themes is developed.

_____  _____  10. Write a review of the book for your school newspaper.

## Prediction Chart

| What characters have we met so far? | What is the conflict in the story? | What are your predictions? | Why did you make these predictions? |
| --- | --- | --- | --- |
| | | | |

# Metaphors and Similes

A **metaphor** is a comparison between two unlike objects. For example, "he was a human tree." A **simile** is a comparison between two unlike objects that uses the words *like* or *as*. For example, "the color of her eyes was like the cloudless sky."

**Directions:** Complete the chart below by listing metaphors and similes from the novel, as well as the page numbers on which they are found. Identify metaphors with an "M" and similes with an "S." Translate the comparisons in your own words, and then list the objects being compared.

| Metaphors/Similes | Ideas/Objects Being Compared |
|---|---|
| 1. <br><br><br> Translation: | |
| 2. <br><br><br> Translation: | |
| 3. <br><br><br> Translation: | |

# Character Chart

**Directions:** In the boxes across from each of the feelings, describe an incident or time in the book when each of the listed characters experienced that feeling. You may use "not applicable" if you cannot find an example.

|  | Lily | August | T. Ray | Rosaleen |
|---|---|---|---|---|
| **Frustration** |  |  |  |  |
| **Anger** |  |  |  |  |
| **Fear** |  |  |  |  |
| **Humiliation** |  |  |  |  |
| **Relief** |  |  |  |  |
| **Empathy** |  |  |  |  |

# Character Attribute Web

**Directions:** The attribute web below will help you gather clues the author provides about a character in the novel. Fill in the blanks with words and phrases that tell how the character acts and looks, as well as what the character says and feels.

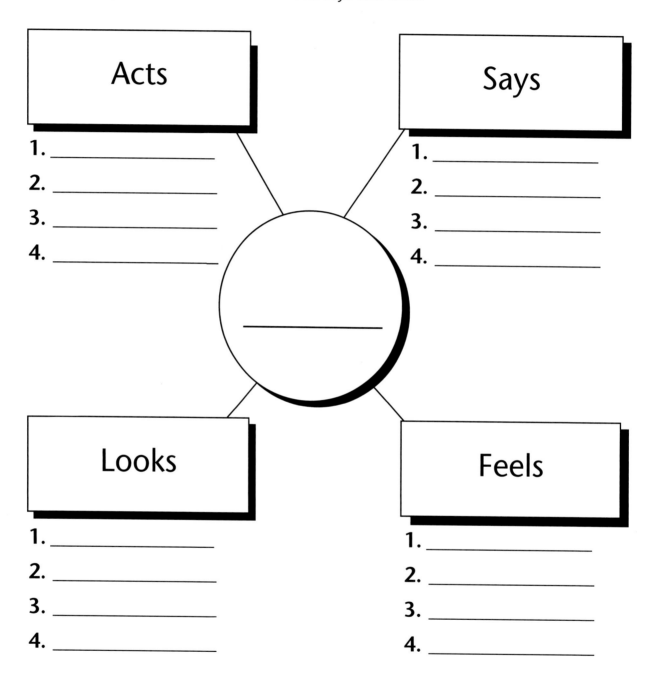

# Herringbone Chart

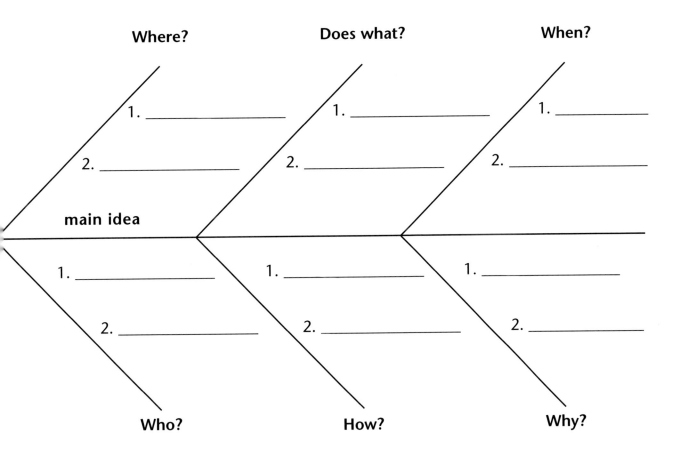

**Where?**

1. _____

2. _____

**main idea**

1. _____

2. _____

**Who?**

**Does what?**

1. _____

2. _____

1. _____

2. _____

**How?**

**When?**

1. _____

2. _____

1. _____

2. _____

**Why?**

# Story Map

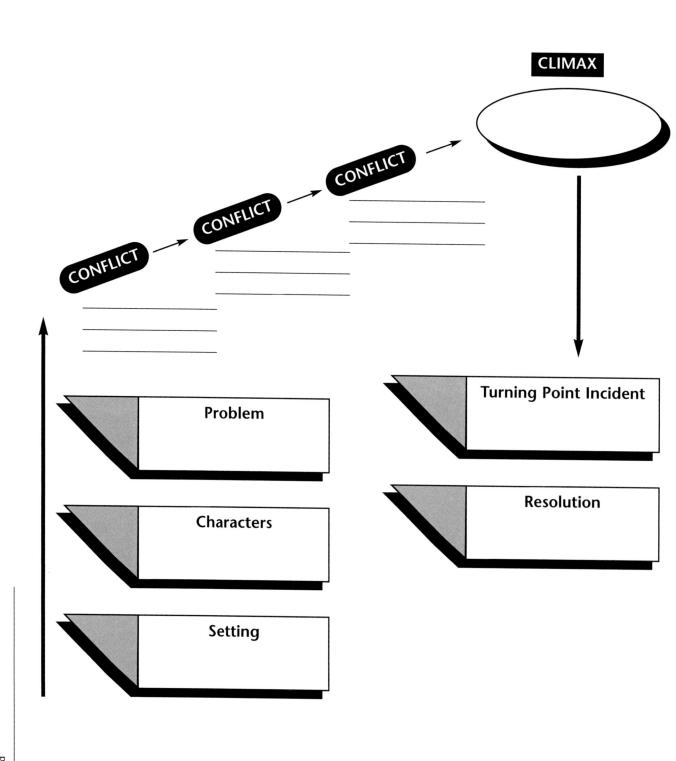

# Vocabulary Card Game

**Teacher Directions:**
- Photocopy and cut out the following pages.
- Give one card to each student in the class.
- The student who has the starred card begins by reading his/her question.
- The student who has the card with the correct vocabulary word responds and then reads his/her question.
- Play continues in this manner until all cards have been read.

| | |
|---|---|
| ☆ **imbecile** <br><br> Who has a word that means showing a false concern for virtue? | **parsonage** <br><br> Who has a word that means defiant or bold? |
| **pious** <br><br> Who has a word that means to follow a winding course? | **brazen** <br><br> Who has a word that means made up from various sources? |
| **meander** <br><br> Who has a word that means the minister's house by the church? | **eclectic** <br><br> Who has a word that means a very stupid or foolish person? |
| **embalm** <br><br> Who has a word that means to search for something? | **trolling** <br><br> Who has a word that means to preserve from decay? |

| industrious | mull |
|---|---|
| Who has a word that means to think about or ponder? | Who has a word that means diligent or hardworking? |

| ingenious | solace |
|---|---|
| Who has a word that means to move sideways or edge along? | Who has a word that means tiny or miniature? |

| deciduous | stamen |
|---|---|
| Who has a word that means craftiness or slyness? | Who has a word that means temper or anger? |

| sidled | minuscule |
|---|---|
| Who has a word that means a place where bees are kept? | Who has a word that means a network of underground galleries? |

| cunning | dander |
|---|---|
| Who has a word that means part of a flower that produces pollen? | Who has a word that means shedding leaves each year? |

| catacombs | apiary |
|---|---|
| Who has a word that means comfort or relief? | Who has a word that means skillful or clever? |

# Linking Novel Units® Lessons to National and State Reading Assessments

During the past several years, an increasing number of students have faced some form of state-mandated competency testing in reading. Many states now administer state-developed assessments to measure the skills and knowledge emphasized in their particular reading curriculum. The discussion questions and post-reading questions in this Novel Units® Teacher Guide make excellent open-ended comprehension questions and may be used throughout the daily lessons as practice activities. The rubric below provides important information for evaluating responses to open-ended comprehension questions. Teachers may also use scoring rubrics provided for their own state's competency test.

*Please note:* The Novel Units® Student Packet contains optional open-ended questions in a format similar to many national and state reading assessments.

## Scoring Rubric for Open-Ended Items

| | |
|---|---|
| **3-Exemplary** | Thorough, complete ideas/information<br>Clear organization throughout<br>Logical reasoning/conclusions<br>Thorough understanding of reading task<br>Accurate, complete response |
| **2-Sufficient** | Many relevant ideas/pieces of information<br>Clear organization throughout most of response<br>Minor problems in logical reasoning/conclusions<br>General understanding of reading task<br>Generally accurate and complete response |
| **1-Partially Sufficient** | Minimally relevant ideas/information<br>Obvious gaps in organization<br>Obvious problems in logical reasoning/conclusions<br>Minimal understanding of reading task<br>Inaccuracies/incomplete response |
| **0-Insufficient** | Irrelevant ideas/information<br>No coherent organization<br>Major problems in logical reasoning/conclusions<br>Little or no understanding of reading task<br>Generally inaccurate/incomplete response |

# Glossary

## Chapter 1

1. presumptuous: acting without permission; too bold
2. paradise: heaven
3. insomniac: a person who is unable to sleep
4. conjure: to bring to mind; recall
5. imbecile: very stupid or foolish person; a person with a weak mind
6. philosophy: a system of principles of conduct, religious beliefs, and/or traditions
7. oblivious: not mindful; forgetful
8. motes: very small particles; specks
9. parsonage: the house provided for a minister by a church

## Chapters 2–3

1. decapitate: to cut off the head
2. brazen: defiant; bold
3. wrench: a tug at one's emotions; a surge of sorrow or anguish
4. pious: religious; showing a false concern for virtue
5. blaspheme: to speak evil of; curse
6. anointed: made holy or purified with oil or similar subtsance

## Chapters 4–5

1. pith: the central spongy tissue in the stems and branches of plants
2. sixth sense: an unusual power of perception; intuition
3. corrugated: shaped into folds or ridges
4. paranoid: irrationally fearful or distrustful
5. meander: to follow a winding course
6. consolation: comfort; reprieve
7. ambrosia: something especially pleasing to taste or smell
8. naive: inexperienced; having a simple nature
9. bona fide: genuine
10. vigilante groups: organizations of Southern white citizens whose aim is to intimidate, oppress, and/or terrorize the black population
11. orthodox: conforming to basic Christian faith
12. eclectic: made up from various sources; broad acceptance of ideas

## Chapters 6–7

1. ingenious: skillful; clever

2. premises: a house or building with its grounds

3. solace: comfort or relief

4. cloister: convent or monastery; quiet place away from the world

5. bordello: house of prostitution

6. consignment: a system by which a dealer pays only for what s/he sells and may return what is unsold

7. mites: tiny, often parasitic arachnids living on animals or plants

8. deciduous: shedding leaves each year


## Chapter 8

1. monogram: a design consisting of two or more interlaced letters, usually a person's initials

2. siesta: a midday or afternoon nap

3. stamen: part of a flower that produces pollen

4. sidled: moved sideways; edged along

5. integrate: to unite or combine; to give equal opportunity and consideration to a group of people


## Chapter 9

1. minuscule: tiny, miniature

2. nymphs: beautiful, graceful Greek and Roman goddesses of nature

3. dander: temper; anger

4. oblivious: not mindful of

5. cunning: craftiness; slyness

6. limbo: a place of confinement; an intermediate place or state

7. animation: liveliness

8. catcall: shrill cry or whistle expressing disapproval


## Chapter 10

1. loping: moving or running with bounding steps

2. induction: ceremony or formal act by which a person is introduced to something; initiation

3. catacombs: network of underground galleries with recesses in which to place the dead

4. taffeta: a smooth, plain-woven fabric with a slight sheen, made of various fibers

## Chapters 11–12

1. industrious: working hard and steadily; diligent
2. mull: think about; ponder
3. sauntered: walked along slowly and aimlessly; strolled
4. exorcism: process of driving out an evil spirit by prayers and/or ceremonies
5. shackled: bound by chains
6. neurotic: suffering from emotional instability; anxious
7. apiary: a place where bees are kept
8. bolstered: supported; propped up

## Chapters 13–14

1. contemptible: deserving scorn; worthless; despicable
2. embalm: to treat a dead body with chemicals to keep it from decaying; preserve
3. melancholy: sad, depressed
4. demoralized: weakened in spirit; lacking courage; confused and disheartened
5. trolling: patrolling an area in search of someone or something

# The Secret Life of Bees

Sue Monk Kidd

## TEACHER GUIDE

### NOTE:

The trade book edition of the novel used to prepare this guide is found in the Novel Units catalog and on the Novel Units website. Using other editions may have varied page references.

Please note: We have assigned Interest Levels based on our knowledge of the themes and ideas of the books included in the Novel Units sets, however, please assess the appropriateness of this novel or trade book for the age level and maturity of your students prior to reading with them. You know your students best!

N 978-1-56137-024-5

To order, contact your
local school supply store, or:

Toll-Free Fax: 877.716.7272
Phone: 888.650.4224
3901 Union Blvd., Suite 155
St. Louis, MO 63115

sales@novelunits.com

novelunits.com

# Table of Contents

# Skills and Strategies

## Comprehension
Predicting, inferring,
cause/effect, conflict

## Literary Elements
Metaphor, simile, symbolism,
irony, allusion, genre,
characterization, theme,
plot development, setting,

## Vocabulary
Target words, definitions,
applications

## Thinking
Brainstorming, analysis,
compare/contrast

## Listening/Speaking
Discussion, monologue,
oral presentation

## Writing
Poetry, point of view, sequel,
time line, essay

## Across the Curriculum
Art—collage, montage;
Drama—script; Music—
ballad, appropriate
selections; Current Events—
articles, research